Oxford English for Cambridge Primary

Workbook

3

Emma Danihel
Izabella Hearn

OXFORD
UNIVERSITY PRESS

Great Clarendon Street, Oxford, OX2 6DP, United Kingdom

Oxford University Press is a department of the University of Oxford. It furthers the University's objective of excellence in research, scholarship, and education by publishing worldwide. Oxford is a registered trade mark of Oxford University Press in the UK and in certain other countries

© Oxford University Press 2016

The moral rights of the authors have been asserted

First published in 2016

All rights reserved. No part of this publication may be reproduced, stored in a retrieval system, or transmitted, in any form or by any means, without the prior permission in writing of Oxford University Press, or as expressly permitted by law, by licence or under terms agreed with the appropriate reprographics rights organization. Enquiries concerning reproduction outside the scope of the above should be sent to the Rights Department, Oxford University Press, at the address above.

You must not circulate this work in any other form and you must impose this same condition on any acquirer

British Library Cataloguing in Publication Data
Data available

978-0-19-836631-7

10 9 8

Paper used in the production of this book is a natural, recyclable product made from wood grown in sustainable forests.
The manufacturing process conforms to the environmental regulations of the country of origin.

Printed in China by Leo Paper Products Ltd

Acknowledgements
The questions, example answers, marks awarded and/or comments that appear in this book and CD were written by the authors. In examination, the way marks would be awarded to answers like this might be different.

The publishers would like to thank the following for permissions to use their photographs:

Cover: Mituaki Iwago/ Minden Pictures/National Geographic Creative; p5: solarseven / Shutterstock; p7: mexrix / Shutterstock; p18: manas_ko / Shutterstock; p20: Ovchynnikov Oleksii / Shutterstock; p23: Vectomart / Shutterstock; p28: dedMazay / Shutterstock; p29: dedMazay / Shutterstock; p30: Yuliia Bahniuk / Shutterstock; p31: Vectomart / Shutterstock; p37: LoopAll / Shutterstock; p41: Klara Viskova / Shutterstock; p44: Galitsyn / shutterstock; p45: Petrovic Igor / Shutterstock; p47: Lorelyn Medina / Shutterstock; p48: joingate / Shutterstock; p50: spom / Shutterstock; p52: Malchev / Shutterstock; p53: dedMazay / Shutterstock; p56: vita khorzhevska / Shutterstock; p57: Malchev / Shutterstock; p58: Lorelyn Medina / Shutterstock; p60: Anton Brand / Shutterstock; p61: Calma Adrian / Shutterstock; p62: Ria Wonder / Shutterstock; p64: zzveillust / Shutterstock; p66: jehsomwang / Shutterstock; p68: Andy Nortnik / Shutterstock; p71: Lorelyn Medina / Shutterstock; p73: lineartestpilot / Shutterstock; p74: Sarawut Padungkwan / Shutterstock; p90: Sarawut Padungkwan / Shutterstock; p92: bigredlynx / Shutterstock

Other artwork is by: Roberta Angaramo, Mark Beech, Q2A Media Services Pvt. Ltd, Claudia Ranucci, Emma Shaw Smith

The author and publisher are grateful for permission to reprint extracts from the following copyright material:

Janine M Fraser: *Abdullah's Butterfly* illustrated by Kim Gamble (Collins, 1998), text copyright © Janine M Fraser 1997, reprinted by permission of HarperCollins Publishers, Australia.

Dahlov Ipcar: 'Fishes Evening Song' from *Whisperings and Other Things* (Knopf, 1967), copyright © Dahlov Ipcar 1967, reprinted by permission of McIntosh & Otis Inc for the author.

Alexander McCall Smith: *Precious and the Monkeys* (Polygon, 2011), reprinted by permission of David Higham Associates on behalf of the author.

Any third party use of this material, outside of this publication, is prohibited. Interested parties should apply to the copyright holders indicated in each case.

Although we have made every effort to trace and contact all copyright holders before publication this has not been possible in all cases. If notified, the publisher will rectify any errors or omissions at the earliest opportunity.

Contents

1. **Fiction** Home and school — 4
2. **Non-fiction** Find out how! — 12
3. **Playscript** Our sensational senses — 20
4. **Fiction** Traditional tales — 28
5. **Non-fiction** Keep in touch! — 36
6. **Poetry** Sharing cultures — 44
7. **Fiction** It's a mystery! — 52
8. **Non-fiction** Our world — 60
9. **Poetry** Why do we laugh? — 68

Writing and vocabulary — 76

Word cloud dictionary — 82

100 High frequency words — 89

New word list — 95

Fiction Reading • Student book pages 10, 11 and 14

1 Home and school

Stories with familiar settings

Abdullah's Butterfly

Read this passage from Abdullah's Butterfly.

"Did you study hard at school today?" asked Abdullah's mother when she came home from the weaving workshop. Because she wants him to do more than weave baskets and catch butterflies for the rest of his life.

"Did you catch me a butterfly today, Abdullah?" asked Grandfather. Because he was hoping to have some of his favourite porridge for tea that night.

Abdullah shook his head.

"It doesn't matter," said Grandfather.

But it did to Abdullah. He thought he would never see another butterfly, so large and beautiful again.

"There is always tomorrow," said Grandfather. "You can always catch me a butterfly tomorrow."…

If he could catch another dragonfly tomorrow, and perhaps a scorpion, and a beetle or two… there would be enough to buy Grandfather the porridge he likes so much.

But not today. There was not time enough left today.

Tomorrow.

From *Abdullah's Butterfly* by Janine M. Fraser and Kim Gamble

4 COPYRIGHT OXFORD UNIVERSITY PRESS 2016. PHOTOCOPYING PROHIBITED

Fiction Reading, grammar and vocabulary • Student book pages 10, 11, 14, 16 and 17

A Now answer these questions about the text.

1 Why did Abdullah's mum want him to work hard at school?
   to gath good bg

2 Do you think Abdullah's grandfather is sad that Abdullah didn't catch a butterfly that day? How do you know?
   no because tmcents all ways tm morw

3 Why was Abdullah sad that he hadn't caught the butterfly?
   _____

B Find verbs in the text which match the following definitions, and fill in the spaces. You might need a dictionary to help you.

1 Grabed to stop something and grasp it.
2 Studs   to work on school work.
3 Bobsled feeling you might get something you want.
4 wave   to twist thread or thin pieces of wood together.

1 Find four adjectives in the text.
   _____   _____   _____   _____

2 Now use the adjectives above to complete these sentences.

   a Abdullah is happy to go to English classes because they are his ___tavitou___ lessons.

   b The scorpion was too ___big___ to fit in the jar.

   c Abdullah's mother works very hard in the ___vagr bg___ workshop.

   d When she was younger, she was a very ___prit___ woman.

COPYRIGHT OXFORD UNIVERSITY PRESS 2016. PHOTOCOPYING PROHIBITED

Fiction Grammar and vocabulary • Student book page 16

Words and sentences

A Draw lines to match these words to their meanings.

noun — a describing word
adjective — an action or doing word
proper noun — a naming word
verb — the name of a particular place or person

B Find the proper nouns in these sentences. Write them in the box below.

1 Anthony grabbed his new satchel.
2 The new student sat next to Amal.
3 Did you see Arnold waiting outside?
4 The journey to Hillside School was long and tedious.

Proper nouns

1	Anthony
2	Amal
3	Arnold
4	Hillside School

C Answer these questions.

1 What is the name of your school?
   nohu hrhe

2 Who goes with you in the mornings?
   mother

3 How do get there?
   I h a cru

4 Describe the journey.
   short 2 sue

6 COPYRIGHT OXFORD UNIVERSITY PRESS 2016. PHOTOCOPYING PROHIBITED

Nouns, adjectives and verbs

A Put the words in the correct order to make sentences. Add capital letters and full stops.

1 book a reads Jamal long
   _____

2 plays happy in puddle a dog the
   _____

3 Emilia window out looks of the dirty
   _____

4 sing bus three on children the little a song
   _____

B Use words from the sentences above to complete these lists.

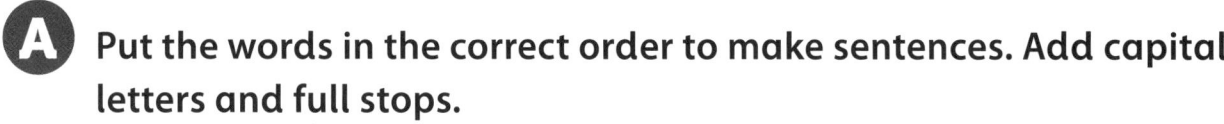

nouns	proper nouns	adjectives	verbs
bus	Emilia	long	sing
___	___	___	___
___		___	___
___		___	___
___			

Fiction Grammar and vocabulary • Student book pages 16 and 17

C Word search

Find 5 nouns, 5 proper nouns, 5 adjectives and 5 verbs.
Use the clues below to help you.

s	w	a	l	k	s	d	n	p	a	j
g	r	a	b	l	a	s	k	s	e	u
c	a	i	r	o	b	b	e	r	r	i
o	d	a	n	c	e	s	l	d	o	c
l	h	a	r	d	n	e	w	a	p	y
d	g	z	s	u	g	a	r	s	l	c
o	n	i	o	n	l	c	e	h	a	l
i	g	j	a	m	a	i	c	a	n	e
f	i	r	e	e	n	g	i	n	e	a
m	a	r	i	a	d	a	v	i	d	n

Nouns
1 f _ _ _   e _ _ _ _ _
2 o _ _ _ _
3 a _ _ _ _ _ _ _ _
4 s _ _ _ _
5 r _ _ _ _ _

Proper nouns
1 J _ _ _ _ _ _ _
2 C _ _ _ _
3 M _ _ _ _
4 E _ _ _ _ _ _
5 D _ _ _ _

Verbs
1 w _ _ _ s
2 g _ _ b
3 a _ _ s
4 d _ _ _ es
5 d _ _ _

Adjectives
1 n _ _
2 h _ _ _
3 c _ _ _
4 j _ _ _ _
5 c _ _ _ _

8 COPYRIGHT OXFORD UNIVERSITY PRESS 2016. PHOTOCOPYING PROHIBITED

Spelling

A These pairs of letters each make one vowel sound: 'ai', 'ea' and 'ou'.

1 Use them to complete the words in the picture boxes.

2 Say the words aloud to hear the vowel sounds.

B Draw lines to make words with two syllables. Write the new words.

por	dow	_____
teach	sect	_____
pan	cake	_____
in	er	_____
win	ridge	_____

C Look at the picture. What can you see? Say each word, listening to the syllables. Write two words that have one syllable and two words that have two syllables.

Fiction Grammar and vocabulary • Student book page 18

Powerful verbs

A Draw lines to connect these powerful verbs with the correct definition.

snatch — cry sadly
sob — eat quickly
beam — move slowly
creep — smile happily
gobble — take suddenly

B Make a list of some verbs that have the same meaning as the verbs in the clouds but are more interesting. One example has been given for you.

creep   dash   gobble

_____   _____   _____
_____   _____   _____
_____   _____   _____

C Write these sentences again using more interesting verbs than 'walk', 'run' and 'eat'.

1   A cat walked up behind a bird.

   _____

2   The man is running for the bus.

   _____

3   Lucy ate her breakfast hungrily.

   _____

Fiction Assessment

Self-assessment on my learning
Unit 1 Home and school

Name _____

Date _____

☺ I understand and can do this well.

😐 I understand but I am not confident.

☹ I don't understand and find this difficult.

Learning objective	☺	😐	☹
Reading fiction skills			
I can find the meaning of unknown words by looking at the words around them.			
I can answer questions by reading a passage and finding the information I need.			
I can understand that characters in stories think one thing, but say a different thing to what they think.			
Writing skills			
I can choose powerful words which make a sentence more exciting.			
I understand how choosing certain words can increase meaning.			
Language skills			
I can collect examples of nouns, verbs and adjectives and use them correctly.			
I can count the number of syllables in words.			
I can spell words that have two vowels together.			

I would like more help with _____

COPYRIGHT OXFORD UNIVERSITY PRESS 2016. PHOTOCOPYING PROHIBITED

Non-fiction Reading • Student book pages 24

Find out how!

Signs and instructions

 A Look at the signs below. Match each sign with a place where you would see it.

| Please remain seated until your name is called | 60 km | Do not touch! |
| | | Flight boarding |

| Pens
Pencils
Crayons
Felt-tips | Raspberries
250 grams | No feeding the animals |
| | | Keep dogs on a lead |

1 In a doctor's surgery
2 Driving along a road
3 In a school classroom
4 In an airport
5 In a supermarket
6 In a museum
7 In a park
8 In a zoo

Non-fiction Reading • Student book pages 26, 27, 30 and 37

B Imagine that you are going to make a cup of tea.

1 What will you need? Place a tick next to the all of the items you will need.

☐ a cup   ☐ a bowl
☐ scissors   ☐ a saucepan
☐ a kettle   ☐ a teaspoon
☐ a fork   ☐ a teabag

2 Here are the instructions to make the tea, but they are not in the correct order. Give the instructions a number and put them in the right order.

Put the teabag in the cup _____

Stir and leave for one minute _____

Find a clean cup _____

Remove the teabag _____

Take a teabag _____

Add milk or sugar to the tea _____

Boil some water _____

Pour the boiled water into the cup _____

C Now rewrite the instructions in the correct order in a paragraph. Use the words below to connect the sentences and to show which order the instructions come in.

first   lastly   then   and   next   after that   and

Example: **First,** find a clean cup **and** take a teabag. **Then**…

_____
_____
_____
_____

Non-fiction Grammar and punctuation • Student book page 33

Commands and questions

A Tick the five command verbs.

put ☐ are ☐ take ☐ ask ☐ who ☐ make ☐ will ☐ throw ☐ then ☐

B Put these words into the correct order to make questions.

1 is Where the cardboard?
_____

2 will produce Who the brightest mask?
_____

3 will colour you paint What the nose?
_____

4 need the we scissors? do Why
_____

5 will you layers of add? tissue paper How many
_____
_____

C 1 Read this text.

It was Clara's birthday at last! The cake was in the oven and Emilia was preparing the sandwiches. It was a warm day so she put the food on the table under the apple tree. Usually it rained on Clara's birthday so the warm weather was a lovely surprise!

2 Add question words to complete the questions about the text. Then answer each question.

<u>What</u> day was it? _____

_____ was the cake? <u>In the oven</u>

_____ prepared the sandwiches? _____

_____ did Emilia put the food outside? _____

Present and past tense

A Circle the ten verbs in the wordsnake.

B Write the verbs from the snake in the past tense.

listened _____

_____ _____

_____ _____

_____ _____

_____

C This is a list of what Oscar planned to do last week. Rewrite each note in the list as a sentence in the past tense saying what Oscar did.

```
Week of May 23rd

1. Visit granny ✓
2. Play football ✓
3. Walk to the park ✓
4. Clean my bike ✓
5. Watch a film ✓
```

1 Oscar visited his _____.
2 He _____ football.
3 _____
4 _____
5 _____

Non-fiction Grammar and vocabulary • Student book pages 29, 32 and 33

Verbs

A Find the 12 hidden verbs that can be used in instructions.

m	i	x	z	x	h	t
a	o	c	i	l	o	a
k	p	u	t	f	l	k
e	m	t	c	k	d	e
f	a	s	t	e	n	p
o	d	i	e	e	o	o
l	d	i	u	p	o	u
d	s	t	i	r	g	r

1 take
2 h_____
3 p_____
4 k_____
5 c_____
6 m_____
7 p_____
8 m_____
9 a_____
10 f_____
11 f_____
12 s_____

B Use some of the verbs above to complete these instructions.

1 _____ your scissors and carefully _____ along the dotted line.

2 _____ off the grass!

3 _____ the milk into the mixture and _____ with a wooden spoon.

C Use the pairs of verbs below to write an instruction.

Example: **Take** two colours and **mix** them together.

1 put/mix _____

2 cut/glue _____

3 take/fold _____

Sentences and questions

A Put these words into the correct order to make a sentence. **Add the correct punctuation.**

1 has brothers older Theo two

_____

2 another can have biscuit I ?

_____

3 Misaki school with to walk I

_____

4 cinema we to see to went the film a

_____

B Add the correct question word to complete these questions.

what   when   where   who   why

1 _____ do you live?
2 _____ does it look like?
3 _____ is your birthday?
4 _____ are you wearing two hats?
5 _____ is going to the park with you?

C Choose two of the question words from above and write your own questions. Don't forget to use the correct punctuation.

1 _____
2 _____

Non-fiction Grammar and spelling • Student book pages 34 and 35

Tenses

A Choose the correct tenses to complete these sentences.

1 He (**was reading/reads**) his book every morning.
2 Nathan (**puts on/put on**) his coat because he was going outside.
3 Malik (**likes/liked**) watching football on TV but Joe does not.
4 Now Lisa (**wore/is wearing**) her favourite blue dress.
5 She (**knew/was knowing**) the answer to the teacher's question.

B Put the verbs in the correct tense.

1 Last night, I _____ (**watch**) a programme about whales.
2 Elephants _____ (**live**) in Africa.
3 When I was little, we always _____ (**visit**) my granny on Saturdays.
4 Kassar _____ (**play**) football after school every day.
5 Peter _____ (**finish**) his homework quickly so he can go out to play.

C The sentences below are in the present tense. Rewrite them changing the present tense to the past tense.

1 She looks everywhere for her dancing shoes.
   _____

2 He walks to school every morning.
   _____

3 He isn't at home because he is playing football in the park.
   _____

Non-fiction Assessment

Self-assessment on my learning
Unit 2 Find out how!

Name _____

Date _____

🙂 I understand and can do this well.

😐 I understand but I am not confident.

☹ I don't understand and find this difficult.

Learning objective	🙂	😐	☹
Reading non-fiction skills			
I can read and follow instructions.			
I can write instructions in order and with connecting words.			
I think about the language used in written instructions and signs.			
I can write questions in order.			
Writing skills			
I can choose the right style for whatever I am writing.			
I think about how information is written on a page.			
I can choose the correct tense.			
Language skills			
I can find examples of nouns, verbs and adjectives and use them correctly.			
I understand that I need to use a verb in a sentence.			
I can add –ed to a verb to make it past tense.			

I would like more help with _____

_____

_____

Poetry Reading • Student book pages 42, 43 and 46

Our sensational senses

Fishes' Evening Song

Read this sound poem out loud.

Flip flop,
Flip flap,
Slip slap,
Lip lap;
Water sounds,
Soothing sounds.
We fan our fins
As we lie
Resting here
Eye to eye.
Water falls
Drop by drop,
Plip plop,
Drip drop.

Plink plunk,
Splash splish;
Fish fins fan,
Fish tails swish,
Swush, swash, swish.
This we wish…
Water cold,
Water clear,
Water smooth,
Just to soothe
Sleepy fish.

Dahlov Ipcar

Poetry Reading • Student book pages 41, 42, 43 and 46

A Answer the comprehension questions below about the poem.

1 Look at lines 1–5 of the poem. Which words describe the sound of water?
_____

2 Who or what is 'we' in lines 7 and 8 of the poem? How do you know this?
_____

3 Some of the words are made-up words. Find the made-up words and write them here.
_____

B Some words sound like the thing that they are describing.
Example: 'whoosh' could describe a firework going through the air.

Find the words in the poem that describe the sound of:

1 water dropping _____
2 a fish moving _____

C Make a list of words to describe as many sounds as you can think of that you might hear at the seaside. You can make some of them up if you want to!

Real words	Made-up words
splash	splosh
_____	_____
_____	_____
_____	_____

COPYRIGHT OXFORD UNIVERSITY PRESS 2016. PHOTOCOPYING PROHIBITED

Poetry Vocabulary and spelling • Student book pages 48 and 49

Prefixes

 A Write the opposite meaning to the words in the cloud using either the prefix *un-* or *dis-*.

___respect   ___kind   ___tidy   ___appear   ___lucky

___dress   ___comfort   ___like   ___necessary   ___order

___trust   ___comfortable   ___popular

Choose 5 of the words above and use each of them in a sentence.

1 _____
2 _____
3 _____
4 _____
5 _____

B Circle the correct words to match the definitions.

1 to make new plans   **prearrange/rearrange**
2 to make plans before   **prearrange/rearrange**
3 to heat before   **preheat/reheat**
4 to reduce the value   **prevalue/devalue**
5 to heat again   **preheat/reheat**
6 to remove bones   **rebone/debone**
7 to change a booking   **rebook/debook**

More prefixes

A Write a definition for these words. You can use a dictionary to help you.

refill _____

retake _____

unhook _____

readdress _____

precook _____

Now write a sentence using each of the words.

1 _____

2 _____

3 _____

4 _____

5 _____

B Choose the correct word from the list below to complete the sentences.

| decode | recapture | depart | preheat | rechargeable |

1 We use _____ batteries, which are more environmentally friendly.

2 You will need to _____ the oven before cooking the cake.

3 Miso's rabbit escaped from its cage, but his mum managed to _____ it.

4 The spy had to quickly _____ the message to understand the clue.

5 We had to hurry because the train would _____ the station in one hour.

Poetry Vocabulary and spelling • Student book pages 48 and 49

Spelling and meanings

A Do these word sums.

1 Un + truthful = untruthful
2 Re + arrange = _____
3 Pre + _____ = prehistoric
4 Dis + like = _____
5 De + _____ = defrost

B

1 Circle the five verbs in this word search.

P	C	O	D	E
R	O	E	M	L
O	O	V	O	O
V	K	E	V	C
E	D	P	E	K

2 Add a prefix *un-, dis-, re-, pre-* or *de-* to each one to make a new word and write them here.

_____ _____ _____ _____ _____

C Rewrite these sentences adding the prefix *un-, pre-* or *dis-* where possible. Make sure you only make real words.

The kind neighbour invited us to view her tidy house. She was very agreeable. Her kitchen was comfortable and organised, and she arranged for us to have cookies – which we liked. That was lucky!

_____
_____
_____
_____

Poetry Vocabulary and spelling • Student book page 41

The senses

 A 1 Nina wrote these sentences about her favourite things for each of the five senses. Read them.

> I love to **see** the stars in the night sky and to **hear** the sound of tinkling water falling in a fountain. I like to **feel** the soft feathers of a fluffy chick, to **smell** fresh toast and to **taste** a juicy orange.

2 Nina planned her sentences using this chart. Complete the chart with ideas of your own. You can draw or write them.

Senses	Nina's ideas	Your ideas
See	stars in night sky	
Hear	fountain	
Touch	chick	
Smell	toast	
Taste	orange	

B Use your ideas to write your own sentences or poem about the senses beginning 'I love to…'.

I love to _____

_____

_____

Poetry Writing • Student book pages pages 41, 42, 43, 44 and 45

Writing poems

1 At the beginning of this unit, you wrote a list of sounds you might hear at the seaside. Do any of your words sound like the things they describe?
Example: crashing waves, squawking seagulls.

Write some more of your own examples here.

_____

2 In the 'Fishes' Evening Song' poem, the writer sometimes repeats the first letter (or first sound) of the words for effect. Can you find some other examples of this in the poem?
Example: plink plunk, splash splish, fish fins fan.

_____

B The writer also uses rhyming words too. Words rhyme when they have the same ending sound.

Example: 'clock' and 'sock' which have the same spelling, or 'door' and 'saw' which have different spellings but the same sound.

1 Find a word in the poem which rhymes with these words.

slap _____ lie _____ drop _____ smooth _____

2 Find three words in the poem which rhyme with the word 'fish'.

_____ _____ _____

C Write your own short poem describing the seaside or another place of your choice. Include some rhyming words and think about the things you might see, feel, hear, smell and taste.

_____

_____

_____

Poetry Assessment

Self-assessment on my learning

Unit 3 Our sensational senses

Name _____

Date _____

☺ I understand and can do this well.

😐 I understand but I am not confident.

☹ I don't understand and find this difficult.

Learning objective	☺	😐	☹
Reading poetry skills			
I can read a range of different poetry and begin to connect ideas.			
I can understand the meaning of difficult words from the context of the sentence.			
I can understand the meaning of a text, as well as what the writer might want me to think about it.			
Writing skills			
I can answer questions about different parts of a text.			
I can use words that sound like the things that they describe.			
I can write a poem.			
Language skills			
I am getting better at using and understanding words with a prefix.			

I would like more help with _____

_____

_____

4 Traditional tales

Why the Bear is Stumpy-tailed

Read this passage from a Norwegian traditional tale.

Once upon a time there was a bear. Back in those days, the bear had a beautiful, long tail and he was very proud of it. One icy cold day the bear met a fox, who came slinking along with a string of fish he had stolen. The bear was very hungry.

"Where did you get all those lovely, juicy fish from?" he asked.

"Oh! Bear," sneered the fox, "I've been out ice fishing and caught them."

"Give me some," begged the bear.

"I tell you what," the fox teased casually, "I'll teach you how to catch your own fish. Then you can have fish any time you want. It's very easy. You've only got to go on the ice, then cut a small hole and stick your long tail down it. You must keep it there as long as you can. You mustn't mind if your tail starts stinging – that's the fish biting. The longer you hold it there, the more fish you'll catch."

"Great," the bear gasped eagerly.

Fiction Reading • Student book pages 56, 57, and 60

A Draw lines to match the words from the story with their correct definitions. Use a dictionary to help you. The first one has been done as an example.

stumpy — not serious
to slink — feel a prick of sharp pain
eagerly — walk in a slow, bendy way
casual — enthusiastically
to sting — short and thick

B Answer the questions using words and phrases from the story to help you.

1 Do you think the fox is telling the truth about catching the fish he is carrying? Explain your answer.
   _____

2 What does the fox say will make the bear's tail hurt in the frozen water?
   _____

3 What do you think will make the bear's tail hurt in the frozen water?
   _____

4 Why do you think the bear is happy to believe the fox's story?
   _____

C

1 Look at the story again. Find three verbs that have been used instead of the word 'said'. _____ _____ _____

2 Write your own sentences using these verbs. You might need to look some of them up in your dictionary.

• _____

• _____

• _____

Fiction Vocabulary • Student book pages 62 and 63

More interesting words for 'said'

A These words can be used instead of for 'said'. Use a dictionary to find out what they mean and then put each word in the correct box. Some words might go in more than one box. *Example:* 'barked' could go in 'said loudly' or 'said angrily'.

bawled	whimpered	mumbled	moaned	bellowed
murmured	grunted	roared	muttered	sighed
raved	screamed	yelled	barked	groaned
thundered	whispered	screeched	wailed	howled

'said loudly'

barked

'said softly'

'said angrily'

barked

B Use one of the words above to complete these sentences.

1 "Get out of my room now!" _____ my brother angrily.

2 "I've hurt my toe," _____ Sofia miserably.

3 "Do you want to know my secret?" _____ Lena.

Fiction Vocabulary • Student book page 62

More synonyms

A Use a thesaurus to find synonyms for the words below.

kind _____   unhappy _____   frightened _____

funny _____   hungry _____   clever _____

B Match a word from the first box with a synonym in the second box.

Example: windy = blustery

windy	beautiful	angry	mumbled	bellowed	stunning
shouted	whispered	brown	**blustery**	chestnut	ancient
old	cold	hot	scorching	enraged	chilly

C Replace the word 'nice' in these sentences with a more interesting synonym.

1 Tessa has (nice) _____ long, blonde hair.
2 The dinner Mum cooked was (nice) _____.
3 Syed is a really (nice) _____ and polite boy.
4 My uncle has a really (nice) _____ new car.
5 It was very (nice) _____ of the girl to give the old lady her seat.
6 Our house is on a (nice) _____ street.

Fiction Punctuation • Student book pages 64 and 65

Speech marks and punctuation

 A Use these words to complete the sentences in the poster.

> first   marks   new   person   spoken   capital   before

Rules to remember!

1. Speech _____ go _____ and after the _____ words.

2. We use a _____ letter for the _____ word of a sentence that is spoken.

3. We use a _____ line when a new _____ speaks.

B Add the speech marks and the correct punctuation to these sentences.

1 Can I come in asked Lucas
   Lucas I can't believe it's you cried Jan

2 Oh no is that a bull howled Barby
   Yes run screeched his sister.

3 Chocolate cake exclaimed Maya
   Would you like some offered Tilly

C Choose one of the scenes above and add two sentences of your own to the conversation.

_____

_____

Writing traditional tales

 Underline all the different words for 'said' in the text below.

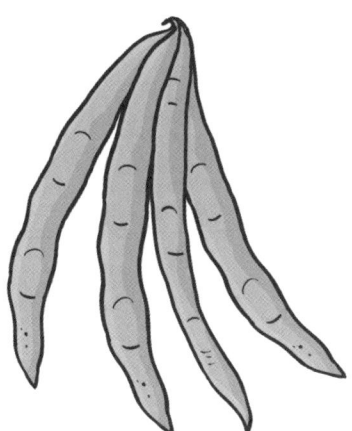

Is the farmer home demanded the man. Maybe I can help suggested the girl. I have these beans to sell explained the man. How much are they asked the girl. I don't want money, I want your horse replied the man. The horse exclaimed the girl. That horse is very old and my beans are special declared the man. That horse is special too argued the girl. Go away and take your beans with you.

B Rewrite the paragraph with speech marks and the correct punctuation. Remember the rules from page 32.

_____
_____
_____
_____
_____
_____
_____

Fiction Punctuation • Student book pages 64 and 69

C Write conversations using the following ideas. Try and use different words for 'said'. The first one has been done for you.

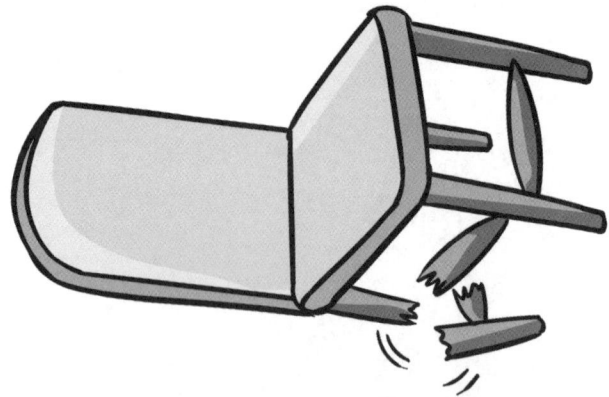

1 Baby Bear is upset to find her chair is broken. Mother Bear says she will mend it.

"Oh no! Look! My chair is broken," cried Baby Bear. "Oh dear!" frowned Mother Bear. "How did that happen? I shall mend it for you."

2 The wolf asks Red Riding Hood where she is going. She explains that she is going to visit her grandmother.

3 The fairy godmother asks Cinderella if she enjoyed the ball. Cinderella describes how she had to run from the ball at midnight.

4 The bear angrily shouts at the fox for tricking him. The sly fox laughs, saying that the bear looks better without his tail.

Fiction Assessment

Self-assessment on my learning
Unit 4 Traditional tales

Name _____

Date _____

☺ I understand and can do this well.

😐 I understand but I am not confident.

☹ I don't understand and find this difficult.

Learning objective	☺	😐	☹
Reading fiction skills			
I can answer questions about different parts of a text.			
I can recognise different types of stories and story themes.			
I can understand the meaning of difficult words by looking at the words around them and the the sentences that they are in.			
Writing skills			
I can use exciting words that make a big impression on the reader.			
Language skills			
I can use synonyms for words that are used very often, like 'said'.			
I can use the correct vocabulary to begin and end a dialogue.			
I can use the correct punctuation and speech marks when using dialogue.			

I would like more help with _____

_____

_____

Non-fiction Reading • Student book pages 72, 73 and 76

Keep in touch!

Letters

Read this letter and then answer the questions.

Dear Mr Cook,

I am writing to complain about the dreadful evening I spent at your restaurant last night.

My son and I were celebrating my 50th birthday. All we wanted was a peaceful evening, eating a delightful meal. However, next to us there was a family with young children making a frightful noise. When I complained, the waiter was useless as he was so fearful of upsetting the parents.

The food was twenty minutes late and it was completely tasteless.

I would therefore be grateful if you consider how you can improve your service in the future.

Yours sincerely,

Mrs B. Brown

Non-fiction Reading, vocabulary and spelling • Student book pages 72, 73, 76, 78 and 79

Comprehension and the suffixes -ful, -less

A Tick one statement that you know is true from Mrs Brown's letter.

☐ The restaurant was very quiet.
☐ The waiter didn't care if he upset the children's parents.
☐ The food tasted really terrible.
☐ The food arrived on time.
☐ Mrs Brown would like some changes to be made to make the restaurant service better.

B Answer the questions about the letter.

1 What is the purpose of this letter?
_____

2 Is it an informal or formal letter? How do you know?
_____

C

1 Make a list of all the words with suffixes used in the letter. Then write another word with the same meaning next to the suffix word. The first one has been done for you.

dreadful _____   terrible _____
_____   _____
_____   _____
_____   _____
_____   _____
_____   _____

2 Now make a sentence using these words.
- successful _____
- endless _____

Non-fiction Vocabulary and spelling • Student book pages 78 and 79

More suffixes

A Read the definitions below and then fill in the missing suffix. The first one has been done for you.

-less or *-ful*

showing good taste	taste**ful**
caring or considerate	thought_____
having no money at all	penny_____
not able to relax	rest_____
very valuable	price_____
to feel upset and angry	resent_____
to have lots of use	use_____
to be very strong	power_____

Don't forget to change 'y' to 'i'.

B The suffix *-ly* is often added to make adverbs. Adverbs describe how something is done. Add *-ly* to the following lists of words.

List 1	**List 2**	**List 3**
careful **carefully**	horrible **horribly**	easy **easily**
bad_____	terrible_____	merry_____
tight_____	idle_____	healthy_____
slow_____	feeble_____	angry_____
clever_____	gentle_____	messy_____

C Read the rules below. Which rule applies to lists 1, 2 and 3 above?

List ____ you take away the **e** from the end of the word and add *-ly*

List ____ you change the **y** at the end of the word to i then add *-ly*

List ____ you simply add *–ly*

38 COPYRIGHT OXFORD UNIVERSITY PRESS 2016. PHOTOCOPYING PROHIBITED

Apostrophes

A Read Mia's letter to her granny and add the missing apostrophes.

B Answer the questions about the letter.

1 What is the purpose of this letter?

_____
_____
_____

2 Is it a formal or an informal letter? How do you know?

_____
_____
_____
_____

Hi Granny,

Were having a great time here in Austria. Ive been skiing every day and cant believe how much Ive improved. I know I shouldnt show off but I think Im even better than Dad now. Hell never admit it though! Were coming home late on Wednesday, so I wont see you until Thursday.

Bye,
Mia

C Write the contractions of the following words.

Example: I have ⇒ I've

She will _____

Can not _____

Was not _____

Did not _____

Must not _____

Do not _____

I am _____

They would _____

Will not _____

He is _____

Non-fiction Grammar and spelling • Student book page 80

Singular and plural nouns

A

1 Add 's' or 'es' to the following singular nouns to make them plural.

church__	table__	watch__	brush__
house__	axe__	class__	dish__
wax__	bench__	chair__	car__
kiss__	beach__	eyelash__	dress__
rock__	hand__	shoe__	cushion__
address__	match__	flash__	floor__
six__	pencil__	spoon__	tax__

2 Look again and complete the sentence below.

> To make them plural, we add 'es' to singular nouns that end in ___, 'sh', ___ or _.

B

Rewrite these sentences, changing the singular nouns to make them plural. The first one has been done for you.

1 The fox sniffed around the house.

<u>The foxes sniffed around the houses.</u>

2 Leave your bag and your torch under the bench.

_____

3 We can explore the beach and then meet on the rock.

_____

4 Pick up your coat and your book and go outside.

_____

5 The girl waited by the gate in front of the shop.

_____

Irregular nouns

A Circle the five nouns in the wordsnake. Write them below.

mousesheepwomanchildperson

_____   _____   _____

_____   _____

B

1 Complete the chart by adding the missing plural or singular word.

mouse	mice
	people
	sheep
	children
woman	

2 Choose the correct word from the chart to complete each sentence below. Read each sentence carefully to check whether the word should be singular or plural.

a The _____ asked his father for an ice cream.

b There were too many _____ in the queue.

c The old _____ was very slow.

d A tiny _____ peeped out of the hole.

e There was a field of _____ in the distance.

C Use three of the plural nouns from above to write interesting sentences of your own.

Example: The mice ate so much cheese that they were full up!

_____

_____

_____

Singular and plural

A Use the picture clues to help you complete the puzzle.

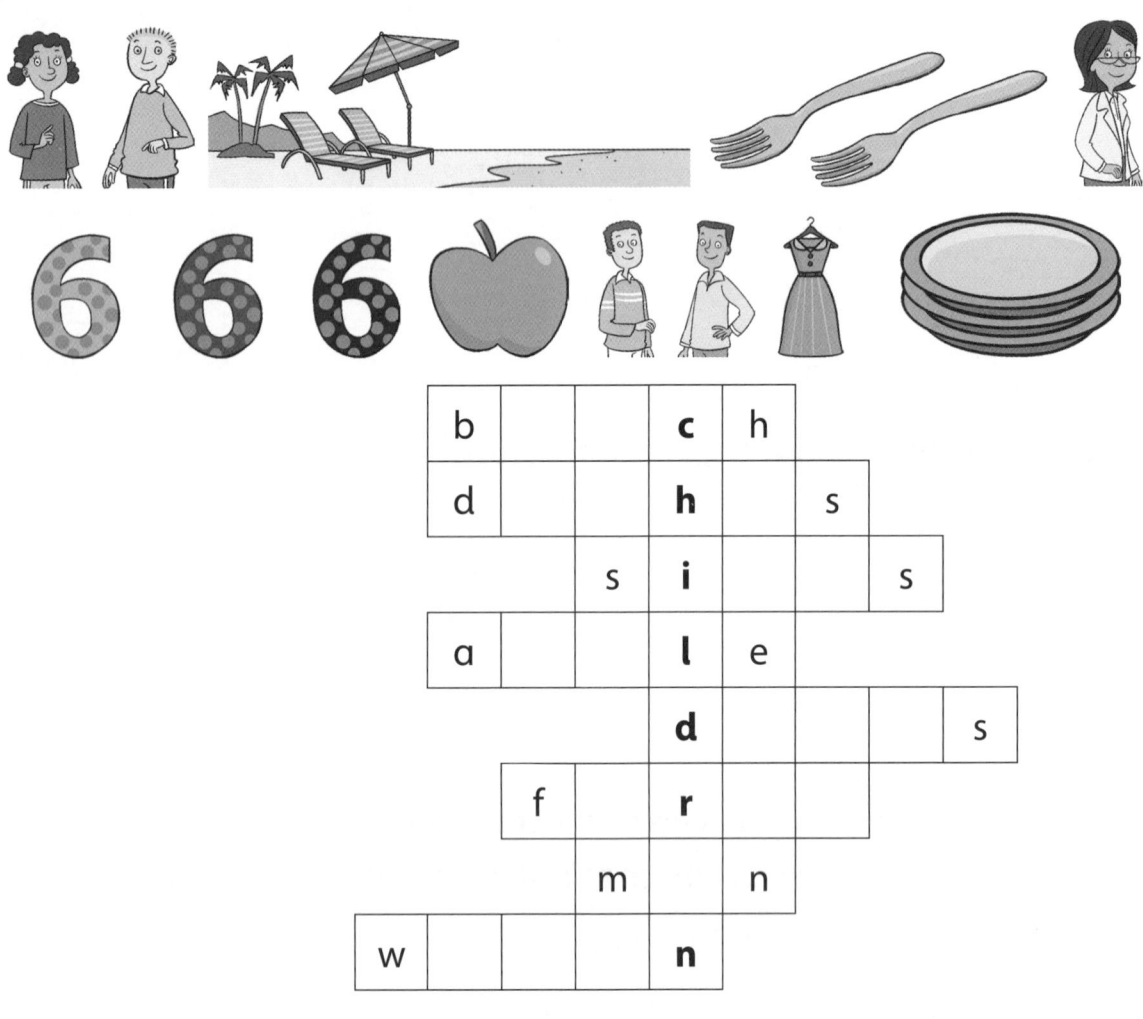

	b			c	h		
	d			h		s	
			s	i			s
	a			l	e		
				d			s
		f		r			
			m		n		
	w			n			

B Copy out the four words that are in the singular and write them in the plural.

Singular   Plural

_____   _____

_____   _____

_____   _____

_____   _____

Non-fiction Assessment

Self-assessment on my learning
Unit 5 Keep in touch!

Name _____

Date _____

☺ I understand and can do this well.

😐 I understand but I am not confident.

☹ I don't understand and find this difficult.

Learning objective	☺	😐	☹
Reading non-fiction skills			
I can read a text and understand what its main purpose is.			
I can scan a passage to find specific information to answer questions.			
Writing skills			
I can understand who I am writing a letter to, and for what reason.			
I can use the correct formal or informal style depending on who I am writing to.			
Language skills			
I can recognise and use different suffixes and prefixes.			
I can use apostrophes in words that have been shortened.			
I understand how to make a word plural.			

I would like more help with _____

_____

_____

6 Sharing cultures

Coyote Steals the Sun

Read this extract from a Zuni legend about the sun and moon.

Coyote lived long, long ago when the world was still dark. There was no sun or moon in the sky. Coyote was a terrible hunter, which he blamed on the darkness. He never managed to catch anything so he was always hungry.

One day he saw Eagle hunting rabbits. Eagle was such a good hunter that he was able to catch many more rabbits than could possibly eat. eat. Coyote immediately thought that if he could hunt with Eagle then he would never be hungry again.

Coyote asked Eagle if they could join together saying that two were surely always better than one. Eagle agreed, so they started to hunt together.

Playscripts Writing ● Student book pages 50, 51, 88, 89 and 92

A Below is the 'Coyote Steals the Sun' story, this time written as a playscript. Use the story on page 44 to complete the dialogue in your own words.

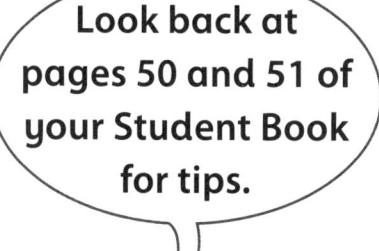

Look back at pages 50 and 51 of your Student Book for tips.

Narrator: Coyote lived long, long ago when the world was still dark. There was no sun or moon in the sky.

Coyote: *(sitting miserably in almost complete darkness)*
Oh, why am I such a terrible _____? I never manage _____ and I'm always _____. If only it wasn't so so _____. Look, *(points sadly)* there is _____ hunting. He is such a good _____. He can catch so many rabbits.

Hmm, *(smiles slyly as he thinks)* I have a plan. If I could only hunt with Eagle then _____ again.

(He calls out) Friend!

(Eagle comes over to where Coyote is sitting.)

B Continue the dialogue by imagining what Coyote and Eagle say to each other in this next part of the story. Include the stage directions.

Eagle and Coyote went hunting together many times, but each time it was the same. Eagle caught a rabbit, Coyote caught nothing. Though he caught nothing, Coyote was greedy and ate twice as much as Eagle. Eagle became tired of hunting for the greedy Coyote. He was cross with Coyote for being such a useless hunter and told him he must try harder.

Coyote: _____

_____

Eagle: _____

_____

COPYRIGHT OXFORD UNIVERSITY PRESS 2016. PHOTOCOPYING PROHIBITED

Alphabetical order

A Put the following words in alphabetical order.

1 coyote   chop   custom   carry   _____
2 eagle   excuse essay   equal   _____
3 dig   dog   dug   deep   _____
4 indeed   invent inform   increase _____

B What can the children see? Complete each sentence by putting the words in alphabetical order. The first one has been done for you.

friendly running five together giraffes.
five friendly giraffes running together.

zebras hungry young stalking lions.

They can see _____

songs parrots colourful singing.

_____

under hippos enormous playing water.

_____

C Make five words from the letters on the dice. Note them in the box. Then write them in alphabetical order.

hat

_____
_____
_____
_____
_____

eat

beach

Poetry and playscripts Grammar and spelling • Student book page 94

Irregular verbs and tenses

A The words below are different forms of the irregular verb 'to be'. Write them in the puzzle.

were   was   are   am   is

B Choose the past tense of the verb 'to be' to fill the gaps.
1. The children _____ waiting for lunchtime to arrive.
2. Rana _____ talking to the teacher at her desk.
3. Kia _____ finishing her class work.
4. She _____ sitting next to Lea.
5. They _____ both wearing hairbands.
6. Joshi and Rao _____ playing chess.
7. I _____ reading a book quietly.
8. Finally, the bell went and the students _____ able to go outside.

C Change these sentences from the past to the present tense.
1. David and Marek were talking about their homework at the bus stop.

   _____

2. I was running very fast because I wanted to catch up with Laura and Maria.

   _____

3. Theo's friends were waiting for him because he was looking for his coat.

   _____

Poetry and playscripts Grammar • Student book page 94

More irregular verbs

A Use a dictionary to find the past tense of these irregular verbs.

awake _____   become _____   bring _____

bite _____   choose _____   freeze _____

know _____   eat _____   rise _____

catch _____   speak _____   hang _____

B Circle all the irregular verbs hidden in the word search. There are 26 altogether.

b	e	f	o	r	g	i	v	e	s
r	c	o	d	r	a	w	i	n	g
e	a	r	i	l	e	a	v	e	s
a	t	g	g	r	e	a	d	w	h
k	c	e	k	n	o	w	p	a	a
g	h	t	s	e	n	d	a	k	n
r	m	l	o	s	i	t	y	e	g
o	a	o	s	p	e	a	k	e	p
w	k	s	e	b	e	n	d	a	u
s	e	e	d	r	i	v	e	t	t

C Choose five of the irregular verbs and write a sentence using each one.

1 _____
2 _____
3 _____
4 _____
5 _____

48 COPYRIGHT OXFORD UNIVERSITY PRESS 2016. PHOTOCOPYING PROHIBITED

Poetry and playscripts Grammar • Student book page 94

Writing and tenses

A Laia comes from Casteldefells, near Barcelona in Spain. April 24th is her favourite day. Read her note and then underline the verbs.

> My best day!
>
> No, it wasn't my birthday, but I knew there were presents in the kitchen. On World Book Day my mum bought me a new book and she got one for Dad too. His was poetry, but she chose a novel for me. He gave her a red rose and I made a card for both of them. We had a delicious breakfast in the cafe across the street. We drank hot chocolate and then we celebrated with the whole street. Everyone exchanged books and flowers.

B Rewrite Laia's note in the present tense. It has been started for you.

No, it isn't my birthday, but I know there are presents in the kitchen. On World Book Day my mum buys _____

C Describe a celebration or event that happens where you live. Use the present tense.

Poetry Writing and spelling • Student book pages 95, 96 and 97

Writing poetry and the alphabet

Read this alphabet poem

My Best Friend

My friend Anna is **amazing**.

She's so **bright** and **clever**,

She is **daring** and **exciting**,

She'll be my **funny** friend forever!

A Now answer the questions about the poem.

1 Which two words rhyme in the poem? _____ _____

2 Look at the bold words and tick the two sentences that are true.

☐ They are all verbs. ☐ They all end with '–ing'.

☐ They all begin with the same letter. ☐ They are all nouns.

☐ They are all adjectives. ☐ They appear in alphabetical order.

B Write as many adjectives as you can to describe a friend or relative. The adjectives could be about their character or what they look like.

_____

_____

C Use your list of adjectives to write the next verse of the poem, describing a friend or relative.

G _____ J _____

H _____ K _____

I _____ L _____

Poetry and playscripts Assessment

Self-assessment on my learning
Unit 6 Sharing cultures

Name _____

Date _____

☺ I understand and can do this well.

😐 I understand but I am not confident.

☹ I don't understand and find this difficult.

Learning objective	☺	😐	☹
Reading poetry and playscripts skills			
I can read a range of poems and playscripts.			
Writing skills			
I can write simple playscripts based on a story.			
I am starting to use tenses properly.			
I can choose words to describe characters.			
I can write a poem.			
Language skills			
I can use irregular forms of common verbs.			
I can organise words alphabetically.			
I can use a dictionary.			
I can choose and compare words to make my writing more descriptive or exciting.			

I would like more help with _____

_____

_____

COPYRIGHT OXFORD UNIVERSITY PRESS 2016. PHOTOCOPYING PROHIBITED

7 It's a mystery!

Adventure and mystery stories

Precious and the Monkeys

Read this extract from Precious and the Monkeys.

They set off, following the path that wound down the hill. It was a narrow path and a winding one – here and there great boulders had rolled down the hill thousands of years ago and the path had to twist around these. In between the boulders, trees had grown up, their roots working their way through gaps in the stone. These trees made the places in between the rocks a cool **refuge** from the heat of the sun, and **sometimes** Precious would sit down there and rest on her way home. But these places were also good hiding places for snakes, and so you had to be **careful** or …

There was a **noise** off among the rocks, and they both gave a start.

"A snake?" whispered Poloko.

"Perhaps," said Precious. "Should we look?"

Poloko nodded. "Yes, but we must be careful."

They heard the noise again. This time Precious thought that it might be coming from the tree, and she **looked** up into the branches.

"There!" she said, pointing into the tangle of leaves.

Poloko looked up. He had expected to see a snake wound round one of the branches, but that was not what he **spotted**.

From *Precious and the Monkeys: Precious Ramotswe's Very First Case* by Alexander McCall Smith

Fiction Reading • Student book pages 102, 103 and 106

A Now answer these questions about the text.

1 Where did Precious sometimes rest on her way home?
   _____

2 Why did she have to be careful?
   _____

3 Where did Precious and Poloko think the noise was coming from?
   _____

4 The noise was not a snake. What do you think it might have been?
   _____
   _____

B Rewrite the sentences and replace the words in bold with 'he', 'they' or 'she'. Look back at the text to help you.

1 **Precious and Poloko** set off, following the path that wound down the hill.
   _____

2 There was a noise off among the rocks, and **Precious and Poloko** both gave a start.
   _____

3 "There!" **Precious** said, pointing into the tangle of leaves.
   _____

4 **Poloko** had expected to see a snake wound round one of the branches.
   _____

C The highlighted words in the extract can be replaced without changing the meaning of the sentence. Use a dictionary to help you find other words to replace the ones in the extract and write them below.

noise _____   careful _____
refuge _____   sometimes _____
looked _____   spotted _____

53

Fiction Vocabulary • Student book pages 101 to 103 and 106

Mystery story vocabulary

A Put the letters in the correct order to find the words. Use the pictures below to help you.

| **tivedetec** de _____ ive | **pfnoisotrt** foot _____ |

| **uecl** c _____ | **mecri** c _____ | **tefih** _____ |

| **rrubgal** b _____ r | **fynimaging agsls** m _____ ing gl _____ |

B Look at the picture story. Use some words above and your imagination to complete the speech bubbles.

Fiction Vocabulary and writing • Student book pages 112 to 115

C

1 Write the story in your own words. Use the pictures to help you plan each part.

_____
_____
_____
_____
_____
_____
_____
_____
_____
_____

2 Choose a title for the story and write it on the cover below. Add an illustration and your name as the author of the book.

Fiction Vocabulary, spelling and grammar • Student book pages 108, 109, 110 and 111

Prefixes and pronouns

Prefixes

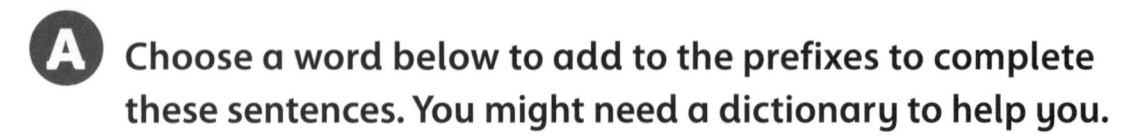

A Choose a word below to add to the prefixes to complete these sentences. You might need a dictionary to help you.

fiction   places   stop   change   pilot

1 Rosie **ex** _____ her teddy for Toby's red truck.
2 Lena ran **non** _____ all the way to school.
3 Gran always **mis** _____ her glasses so now she keeps them around her neck.
4 Florian's father is the **co** _____ of a jumbo jet.
5 Laura enjoys reading **non** _____, especially biographies.

B Write sentences using the following words.

1 nonsense _____
2 misunderstand _____

Pronouns

A Complete the sentences by adding the correct pronoun.

1 My mother told _____ to clean up my room.
2 Joel picked up his book and then _____ began to read aloud.
3 As the children were being so loud, the teacher told _____ to be quieter.
4 Sofie's best friend gave _____ a lovely birthday present.
5 The boys put on their coats and then _____ went outside to play.
6 We were thirsty so Mum gave _____ a drink with our lunch.

B Make your own sentences using these pronouns.

1 she _____
2 them _____
3 it _____

Writing adventure stories

Read this adventure story.

Fred and Fred's little brother, Nathan, stood in the middle of the empty, ruined castle, outside the doorway to the completely black dungeon room.

"Nathan **dares** Fred to go in," whispered Nathan. Fred was shaking because Fred felt so terrified but Fred did not want Fred's little brother to know that Fred was frightened, so Fred grabbed Nathan's hand and said, "Fred will only go in if Nathan **comes** with Fred."

"OK. Nathan will come," said Nathan.

Together Fred and Nathan edged into the darkness. Fred felt Fred's heart beating so fast…. at least Nathan was with Fred. Further and further in Fred and Nathan went.

A Rewrite the story. Add the correct pronouns to replace the underlined words and then change the verb forms in bold if you need to.

Fiction Writing • Student book pages 112, 113, 114 and 115

B Read these statements about writing adventure stories and decide whether they are true or false. Draw a circle around the correct answer.

It is bad to describe the setting.	**True / False**
It is good to include dialogue.	**True / False**
It is good to always use short sentences.	**True / False**
It is bad to talk about how the main character feels.	**True / False**
It is good only to describe what the main character sees.	**True / False**
It is good to build up tension and to have some exciting action.	**True / False**
It is good to have a plot leading to a dramatic climax.	**True / False**
It is bad for the main hero to solve the problem at the end.	**True / False**
It is bad to use powerful adjectives.	**True / False**

C Write a more powerful adjective or verb next to the following words.

good _____
scary _____
horrible _____
smelly _____
shout _____
loud _____
crying _____
take _____
run _____

58 COPYRIGHT OXFORD UNIVERSITY PRESS 2016. PHOTOCOPYING PROHIBITED

Fiction Assessment

Self-assessment on my learning
Unit 7 It's a mystery!

Name _____

Date _____

☺ I understand and can do this well.

😐 I understand but I am not confident.

☹ I don't understand and find this difficult.

Learning objective	☺	😐	☹
Reading fiction skills			
I can understand the meaning of difficult words by looking at the words around them and at the sentences that they are in.			
I can identify the features of different types of stories.			
Writing skills			
I can use exciting words that make a big impression.			
I can use words to make my writing more descriptive.			
I can plan the parts of a story I am writing.			
Language skills			
I can use a dictionary.			
I can use pronouns correctly in sentences.			
I can use correct verb forms with different pronouns.			
I can use a range of prefixes and suffixes.			

I would like more help with _____

_____

_____

Non-fiction Reading • Student book pages 118, 119 and 122

8 Our world

Non-chronological reports

A Read this report about the Arctic, then think of a title and three subheadings. Write them in the spaces provided.

[Title] _____

[Subheading 1] _____

The Arctic is an area at the northernmost part of the Earth. As well as the Arctic Ocean, this huge region includes parts of Russia, Greenland, Canada, the USA, Norway, Iceland, Sweden and Finland.

[Subheading 2] _____

The Arctic has cold winters and cool summers. The average winter temperature is −40 degrees Celsius. The coldest recorded temperature, measured in the Siberian village of Verkhoyansk, is −68 degrees Celsius. However, global warming is rapidly shrinking the amount of ice on the Arctic Ocean.

[Subheading 3] _____

People have lived in this frozen region since 2500 BCE. The Inuit people living in the north west of Greenland are one of the most northern communities in the world. Most Inuit communities have settled along the coastline as these people depend on the sea to survive.

Non-fiction Reading • Student book pages 118, 119 and 122

B **Answer these questions using the information in the report.**

1 The Arctic region includes parts of many different countries. Name five of them.
   _____

2 What is the coldest temperature recorded in the Arctic region?
   _____

3 Why is there less and less ice each year in the Arctic region?
   _____

4 What is the name given to one of the groups of people who live in the most northern communities?
   _____

5 Tick one box to show which statement is true.
   ☐ People living in the Arctic mostly live inland because it's warmer.
   ☐ The coldest temperature on record was measured in Greenland.
   ☐ People have lived in the Arctic region since 2500 BCE.

C **Does this report contain mostly facts or mostly opinions? Explain your answer.**
   _____

Non-fiction Grammar and spelling • Student book page 124

Irregular verbs

A Complete these sentences with the correct verb form of 'to have' or 'to go'.

1 This morning Felix _____ to the dentist because he _____ toothache.

2 My neighbours _____ a lovely time last year when they _____ on holiday to Spain.

3 She _____ an uncle living there, so they _____ to Spain every year.

B Rewrite these sentences in the present tense.

1 She had a new bicycle so she often went for a ride.
   _____

2 I had an ice-cream when I went to the seaside.
   _____

3 The boys had swimming lessons on Wednesdays so they went to the pool by bus.
   _____
   _____

C Use your own ideas to finish the sentences below. Use the verbs 'to have' or 'to go' in the past tense. Make the sentences as interesting as possible.

1 Jenna's hobby was skateboarding, so
   _____

2 Mum doesn't like cooking, so
   _____

3 Every Saturday, Pablo and his friends
   _____

Non-fiction **Vocabulary** • Student book page 125

Compound words

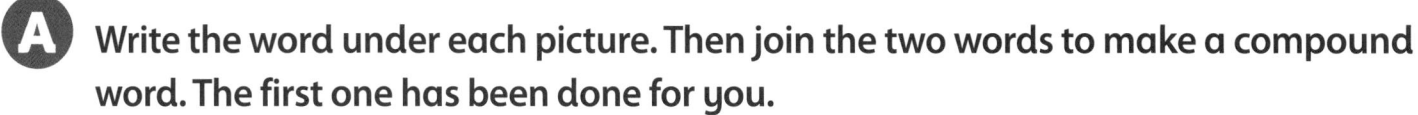

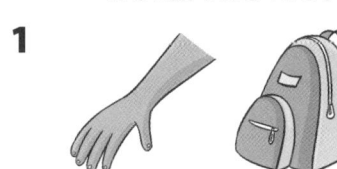

A Write the word under each picture. Then join the two words to make a compound word. The first one has been done for you.

1 hand + bag = handbag

2 _____ + _____ = _____

3 _____ + _____ = _____

4 _____ + _____ = _____

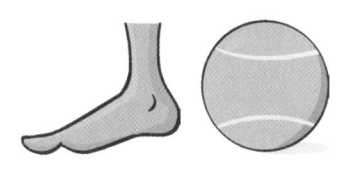

B Each picture shows a compound word. Write the compound word and then split it into its two parts. The first one has been done for you.

1 keyboard = key + board

2 _____ = _____ + _____

3 _____ = _____ + _____

4 _____ = _____ + _____

C Choose two compound words from activities A and B and use them in a sentence.

_____

Non-fiction Grammar, spelling and vocabulary • Student book pages 126 and 127

Simple and compound sentences

A Add the correct connective (and, so, but) to complete these compound sentences.
1 Alba was very tired _____ she went to bed early.
2 I like most vegetables _____ I don't like peas.
3 Emil likes literacy _____ he likes numeracy.
4 Milan has been to India _____ he has never been to Pakistan.
5 Diego missed the bus _____ he had to get a lift to school from his father.

B Join these sentences together using a connective to form a compound sentence.
1 Leo kicked the ball at the net. He didn't score a goal.
   _____
2 Mathew didn't have anything to write with. I gave him a pencil.
   _____
3 Julia likes ball games. She doesn't like running.
   _____
4 Hassan loves running. He is the fastest boy in the class.
   _____
5 I was feeling sick. The teacher phoned my mother to pick me up from school.
   _____

C Complete these sentences with an idea of your own.
1 Lena wanted to go to the beach so _____.
2 Louis has three brothers but _____.
3 Patrik isn't very good at swimming but _____.
4 My grandmother is a great cook so _____.
5 Clara went to Portugal on holiday with her family and _____.

Vocabulary and connectives

A

1 Fit the words listed below into the puzzle.

cubs desert carnivorous pride

```
    m
  s
  e
    d
  k
  r _ _ _ _ _ _ _
  t
c
```

2 Which animal name is made when the puzzle is complete? _____

B Write the correct word from activity A next to each definition.

1 _____ : young lions
2 _____ : animals that live in the Kalahari Desert in South Africa.
3 _____ : meat (flesh) eating.
4 _____ : a dry, sandy place.
5 _____ : a group of lions.

C Underline the connectives in these unfinished sentences. Then complete the sentences using information from activity B.

1 Lions eat meat but not all animals are_____.
2 Lions live in groups called _____ and their young are _____
   _____.
3 Meerkats do not live in a forest but _____
   _____.

Non-fiction Grammar and punctuation • Student book page 127

Clauses and commas

A Underline the main clause in the following sentences.
1. Before getting dressed, Ravi cleaned his teeth.
2. After school finished, Susan went to play at Millie's house.
3. When his mother came in the room, Khan was fast asleep.
4. Before slamming the door, Freda grabbed her coat.
5. When Enzo got up, he couldn't believe it was snowing!

B Complete these sentences with your own ideas and put a comma in the correct place.
1. Before picking Juan up from school his mother _____

2. Although Flora loved going to stay at her cousin's house she didn't _____

3. After Euan had finished his dinner he _____

4. When Alexander went to the park he was surprised to _____

5. As Norma was leaving the house her mother _____

C Look at the report on the Arctic again on page 60. Find two sentences where a subordinate clause has been used. Write them out below.
1. _____.
2. _____.

Non-fiction Assessment

Self-assessment on my learning
Unit 8 Our world

Name _____

Date _____

☺ I understand and can do this well.

😐 I understand but I am not confident.

☹ I don't understand and find this difficult.

Learning objective	☺	😐	☹
Reading non-fiction skills			
I can scan a passage to find specific information to answer questions.			
I can understand the main point of a text.			
Writing skills			
I can recognise the features of an information text.			
I am beginning to organise my writing in paragraphs.			
I am thinking about how information is set out on a page.			
I am improving my use of tenses.			
Language skills			
I know irregular forms of common verbs.			
Use and spell compound words.			
I can use simple, compound and complex sentences.			
I can use commas.			

I would like more help with _____

_____

_____

Poetry Vocabulary and spelling • Student book page 140

9 Why do we laugh?

Dictionary work

A Look up these verbs in a **dictionary** then draw a line to match them with their correct definition.

snigger	come down from the air suddenly
mutter	make a quick, sharp cry
snatch	laugh in a rude, disrespectful way
yelp	take suddenly
swoop	complain quietly

B Use the verbs above to complete this story. You will need to put the verbs in the past tense.

We were sitting in the park one sunny day having a family picnic. Suddenly a seagull _____ down from nowhere and _____ the cheese sandwich straight out of my hand. I _____ in shock.

My big brother looked at my empty hand and _____.

"Just look at your face!" he laughed.

"Leave me alone," I _____ angrily, but he just kept on laughing.

C Put these words in the order you would find them in a dictionary.

detail   dusty   dwell   door   damp   dare   dye   drop

1st <u>damp</u>   2nd _____   3rd _____   4th _____
5th _____   6th _____   7th _____   8th _____

Thesaurus work

A Use a **thesaurus** to match the words in the clouds to the word that they could replace. Fill in the lists below.

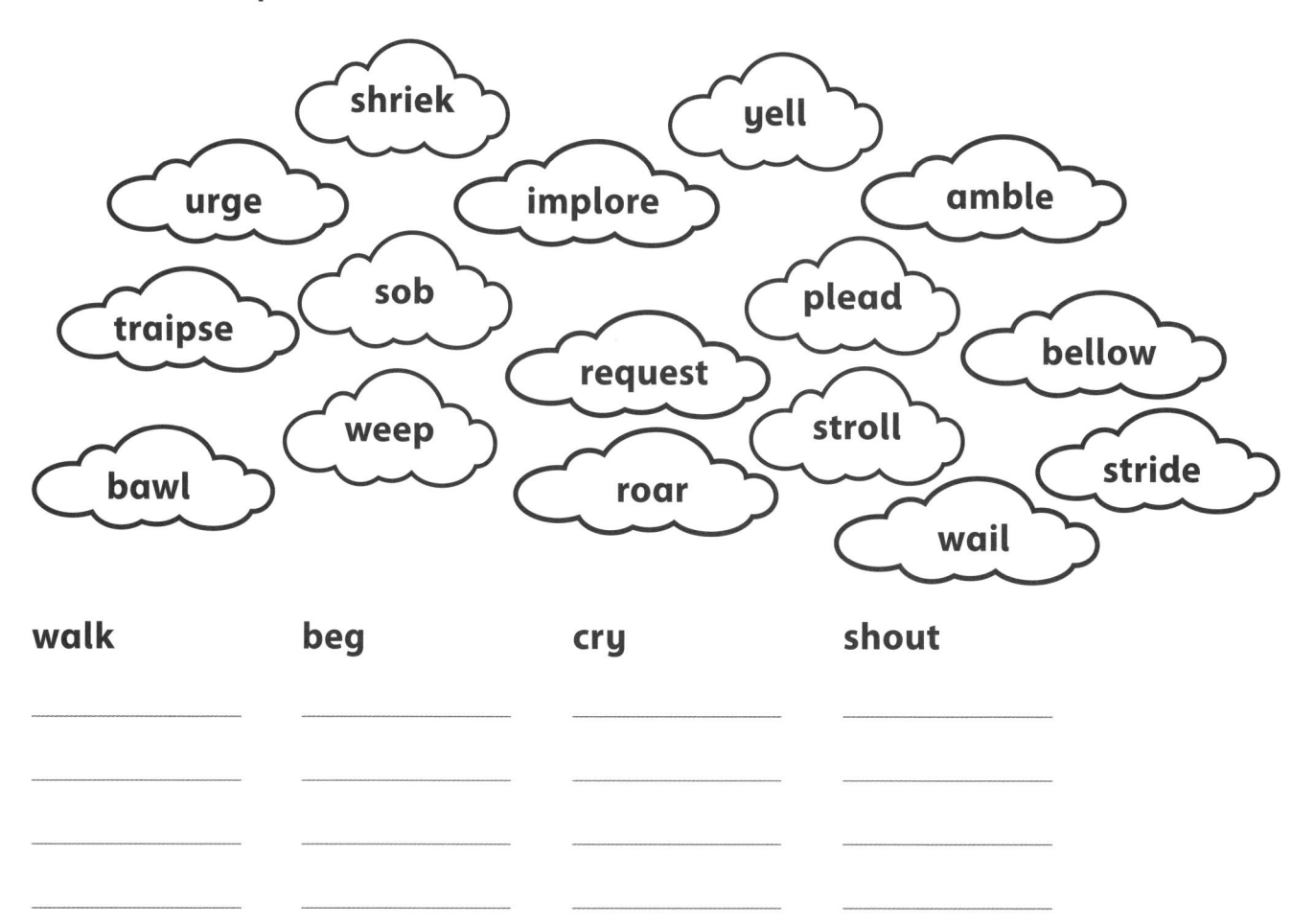

shriek, yell, urge, implore, amble, sob, plead, traipse, bellow, request, weep, stroll, bawl, roar, stride, wail

walk	beg	cry	shout
_____	_____	_____	_____
_____	_____	_____	_____
_____	_____	_____	_____
_____	_____	_____	_____

B Choose one of the words from your lists in the previous exercise to replace the word in brackets and complete these sentences. Remember to use the past tense.

1 Leonard _____ (**walk**) home from school feeling happy that it was Friday.

2 "Please, please, please may I have a puppy," Kia _____ (**beg**) her mum.

3 "You are not going anywhere until you have cleaned your room," _____ (**shout**) my dad.

4 "You've eaten all my birthday cake," _____ (**cry**) my little sister.

Non-fiction Vocabulary and spelling • Student book page 140

Vocabulary and alphabetical order

A

1 Complete each word below by adding the missing letter. Use a dictionary to help you.

   po_try   nar_ative   s_llable   ho_onym   laug_

2 Use all the letters you added to make a new word. **Clue:** Limericks use this.

   _____

B Dieter is writing a dictionary. Page 11 will include all words in alphabetical order from 'blue' to 'brown'. He has circled the two words in his list that will also appear on page 11.

Dictionary page	Word list
Page 11 blue – brown	(break), burn, (boy), bee

Circle the two words that should appear on page 34 and do the same for page 40.

Dictionary page	Word list
Page 34 safe – sound	smug, star, sad, soldier
Page 40 whale – write	wait, why, window, weep

C

1 Make as many words as you can from the word wheel. Always use the middle letter. Write them in alphabetical order.

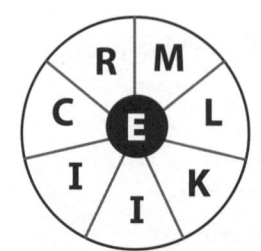

   Word wheel letters: R, M, C, L, I, K, I, with E in the middle.

   _____
   _____
   _____

2 Which word can you make using all the letters? _____

Dictionary work and homonyms

A Look in the dictionary and find three different meanings of the word 'bark'.

Some homonyms are spelt differently but are pronounced the same.

Example: read, red

1 _____
2 _____
3 _____

B Find a homonym for these words from the words in the clouds on page 69.

raw _____

ball _____

whale _____

C Write a homonym to match these words. Use a dictionary to help you.

knew _____   hear _____   write _____

hole _____   meet _____   there _____

two _____   through _____ no _____

Non-fiction Vocabulary and spelling • Student book page 141

More homonyms

A

1 Draw lines to link the pairs of homonyms. One pair has been found for you.

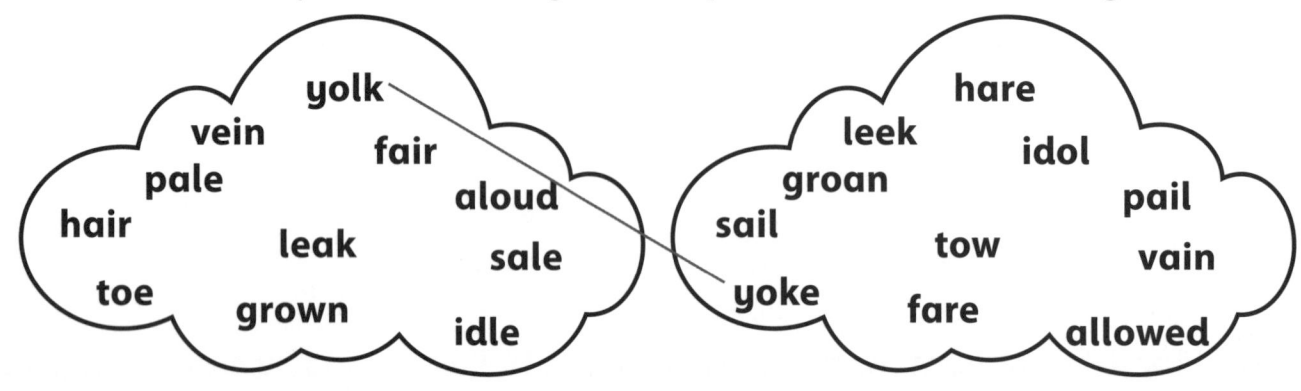

Cloud 1: yolk, vein, fair, pale, aloud, hair, leak, sale, toe, grown, idle

Cloud 2: hare, leek, idol, groan, sail, pail, tow, vain, yoke, fare, allowed

2 Write each pair in the correct place on the alphabet chart.

A	G	M male	S
B bee	H	N nose knows	T
C cell sell	I	O one won	U urn earn
D dye	J jeans genes	P	V
E ewe you	K key quay	Q queue cue	W wail
F	L	R reign	XXXXXXXXX Y ZZZZZZZZZZ

B
Two homonyms may begin with a different letter. Find examples of these in the chart and underline the letters they begin with.

C
Complete the chart by writing homonyms for the words in bold. Use a dictionary to help you. There are no homonyms for X and Z!

Writing a limerick

A Choose a word from the words in bold to fill the gaps and complete the two limericks.

1 **tomatoes   grass   packet   sorry
Leeds   lass*   seeds   covered**

[* **lass** is another word for girl]

There once was a young lady from _____,

Who swallowed a _____ of _____.

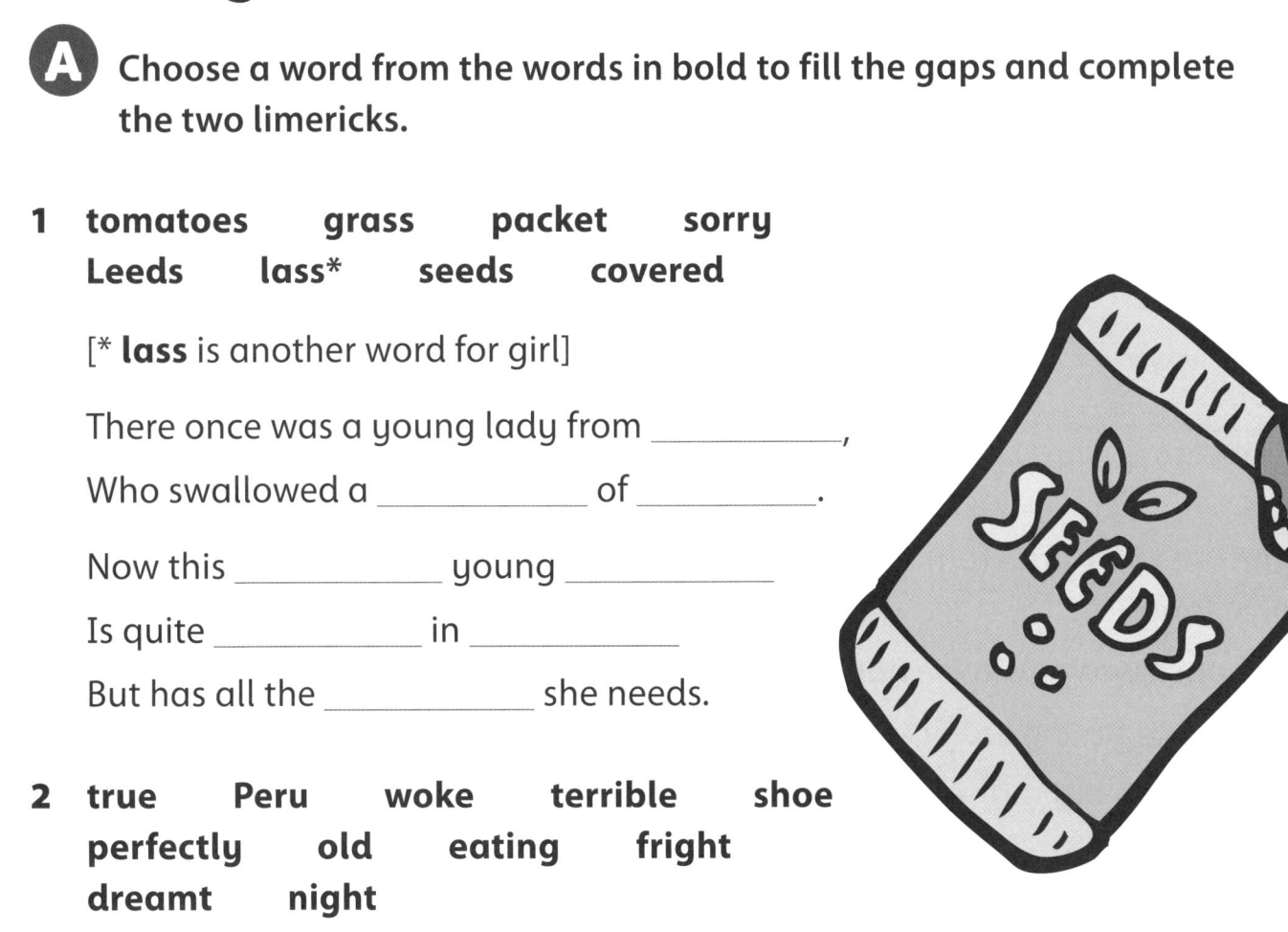

Now this _____ young _____

Is quite _____ in _____

But has all the _____ she needs.

2 **true   Peru   woke   terrible   shoe
perfectly   old   eating   fright
dreamt   night**

There was an _____ man of _____,

Who _____ he was _____ a _____.

He _____ up one _____

With a _____ _____

And found out it was _____ _____.

Poetry Writing • Student book pages 142 and 143

B **Think of a way of completing this limerick using the rhyming words 'hour', 'flower' and 'weeds' at the end of the lines.**

There was a wee* toddler from Leeds,

Who swallowed a packet of seeds.

_____

_____

_____

[*wee is another word for small.]

C **Choose *one* of the following opening lines and use it to write your own limerick.**

1 There once was a tortoise named Fred
2 There was a young lady called Sue
3 There was an old farmer from Wales
4 There was a poor girl in a hat

_____

_____

_____

_____

Poetry Assessment

Self-assessment on my learning
Unit 9 Why do we laugh?

Name _____

Date _____

☺ I understand and can do this well.

😐 I understand but I am not confident.

☹ I don't understand and find this difficult.

Learning objective	☺	😐	☹
Reading poetry skills			
I can read a range of poetry.			
Writing skills			
I am getting better at choosing tenses.			
I can write and perform poems, thinking about the sound of words.			
Language skills			
I can use a dictionary to find the meaning of words.			
I can put words in alphabetical order using the first two letters.			
I can find synonyms for words.			
I can use powerful adjectives and verbs.			
I can find words that have the same spelling but a different meaning.			

I would like more help with _____

_____

_____

Writing and vocabulary

Writing a traditional tale

A Look at the picture story and find out what can happen if we do something without thinking!

Think before you act!

Writing and vocabulary

B **Write the picture story in your own words.**

1 Start by describing the setting. Where does the story take place? What time of year is it? What's the weather like? Remember to use strong adjectives and interesting verbs as well as noun phrases. Write about each picture in order.

2 Add a title to the story.

Title _____

Writing and vocabulary

Writing an adventure story

A Matilda and Ricardo were taking their dog for a walk when they stumbled across something very interesting! Look at the picture story.

Writing and vocabulary

B Imagine you are one of the children. Write about what happened from their point of view. Remember to write about each picture in order.

C What do you think happens next? Imagine the conversation the children have with their parents when they get home. Write a short dialogue between the children and their mother and father. The dialogue has been started for you.

Remember to use correct punctuation and a variety of interesting synonyms for 'said'. You can use the words in the box or write your own.

| gasped | explained | asked | screeched | muttered | howled |
| yelled | mumbled | sighed | bellowed | | |

"Mum, Dad!" cried Matilda as she rushed through the door.

Writing and vocabulary

Vocabulary
Word fun

A Each picture is a clue to a word in the wordsearch. Find the seven words.

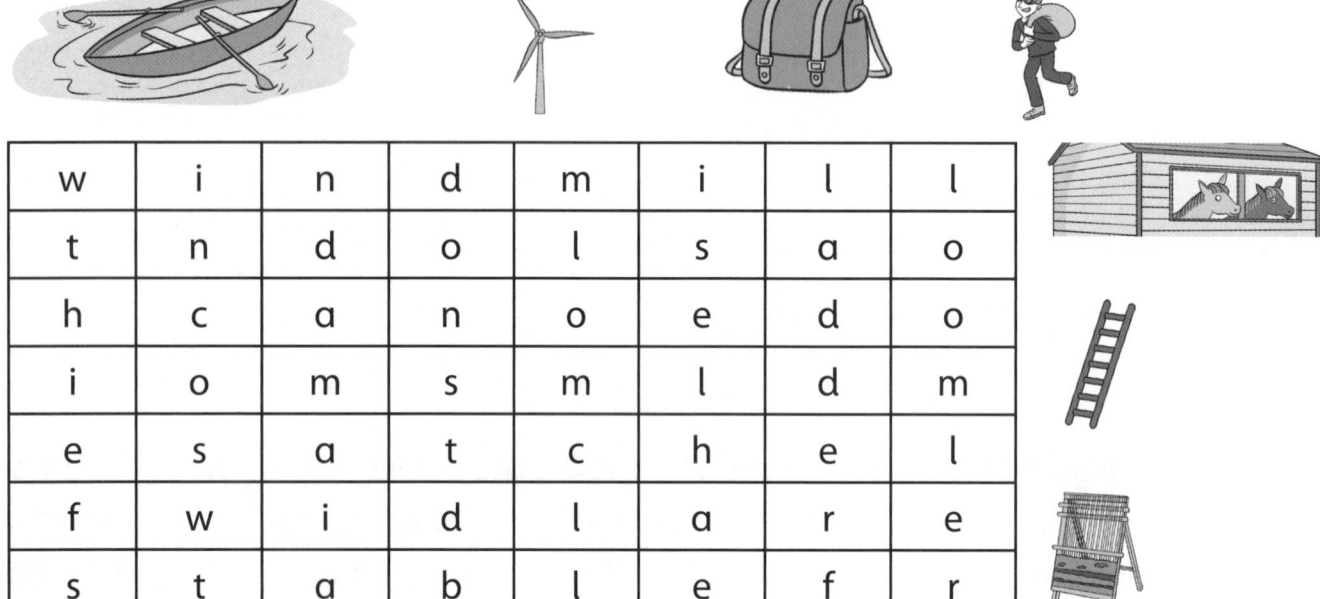

w	i	n	d	m	i	l	l
t	n	d	o	l	s	a	o
h	c	a	n	o	e	d	o
i	o	m	s	m	l	d	m
e	s	a	t	c	h	e	l
f	w	i	d	l	a	r	e
s	t	a	b	l	e	f	r

B Write the words from the wordsearch in the correct places and then complete the definitions. Use the Word cloud dictionary on pages 82–88 to help you.

_____loom_____ : a machine for _____ cloth

_____ : a small, narrow _____ with a paddle

_____ : a _____ with sails

_____ : a _____ for carrying books

_____ : _____ who steals

_____ : a _____ for horses

_____ : something you can _____ to reach high up

C Write a number next to each word to put them in alphabetical order. (1 being the first in alphabetical order and 7 the last)

80 COPYRIGHT OXFORD UNIVERSITY PRESS 2016. PHOTOCOPYING PROHIBITED

Writing and vocabulary

Verbs

A Find the 12 verbs in this wordsnake. The first one has been found for you.

laughgaspburrowpeersquealpantslipgrizzlesnatchhowlnibbletricklepeck

B Choose a verb from the snake to complete the sentences. You will need to write the verb in the past tense.

1 The water _____ out of the pipe.
2 The rabbits _____ their way under the fence.
3 The birds _____ at the ripe fruit on the tree.
4 The children _____ at the joke.

C Write a sentence describing each picture. Use the verbs provided. You can change the tense. The first one has been done for you.

nibble   peer

She peered into the kitchen as the girl nibbled the biscuit.

snatch   squeal

_____

gasp   slip

_____

Word cloud dictionary

Aa
adamantly *adverb* do or say something in a way that shows you are determined or have a strong opinion
achieve *verb* succeed in doing something
address *noun* your address is where you live
adventure *noun* a strange, exciting or dangerous event or journey
air mail *noun* letters and parcels that are carried by aircraft
ajar *adjective* partly open
amusing *adjective* making you laugh or smile
Arctic *noun* the area round the North Pole
authority *noun* the power to give orders

Bb
boarding school *noun* a school where children are able to live during term time
burrow *verb* dig a hole under the ground

Cc
canoe *noun* a light, narrow boat that you move by using a paddle
cardboard *noun* very thick, strong paper
climber *noun* someone who climbs hills and mountains for sport
compost *noun* a mixture of rotten stalks, leaves and grass
creator *noun* someone who creates or makes something
creep *verb* move along quietly and slowly with the body close to the ground

Word Cloud dictionary

crumb *noun* a very tiny piece of bread or cake

culture *noun* all the traditions and customs of a group of people such as art, music, literature, science and learning

cyclist *noun* a person who rides a bicycle

Dd

danger *noun* the chance that something bad might happen or someone might get hurt

decoration *noun* an object that is added to make something look more beautiful or colourful

detective *noun* someone who looks at clues and tries to solve a mystery or find out who committed a crime

downstream *adverb* in the direction that a river or stream flows

drain *noun* a pipe or ditch for taking away waste, water or sewage

Ee

elastic band *noun* a band made of stretchy material, used to hold things in place

elegant *adjective* graceful or tasteful

enquiry *noun* a question you ask when you want information

exaggerate *verb* say that something is bigger, better or more important than it really is

Ff

festival *noun* a special time when people celebrate something

flavour *noun* the taste of something that you eat or drink

Word Cloud dictionary

frond *noun* a large leaf, which is made up of lots of smaller leaves, such as the leaf of a fern plant
frozen *adjective* something that has turned to ice
frustrate *verb* prevent someone from doing something or from succeeding in something

Gg
gasp *verb* breathe in suddenly when you are shocked or surprised
glue *noun* a sticky substance that you use for sticking or holding things together
greet *verb* welcome someone and say hello to them
grill *noun* a device for cooking food, which uses a flame or a glowing element
grizzle *verb* sulk, grumble or whine
grub *noun* an animal that looks like a small worm and will become an insect when it is an adult

Hh
haul *verb* pull or drag something along
howl *verb* make a long, high sound, like the sound of an animal crying or a strong wind blowing
hunt *verb* chase and kill animals for food or as a sport

Ii
instruction *noun* an order or piece of information that tells you what to do

Jj
joke *noun* something you say or do to make people laugh
journey *noun* when you go on a journey, you travel somewhere

Kk
kiln *noun* a type of oven or furnace

Ll
ladder *noun* a tall frame you can climb to reach something high up
launch *verb* took off into the air
laugh *verb* make a noise or sound that shows you are happy or think something is funny
legend *noun* an old story that has been handed down from the past
limerick *noun* a funny poem with five lines and a strong rhythm
loom *noun* a machine for weaving cloth

Mm
Maori *noun* a member of the aboriginal people of New Zealand
master *noun* a male teacher
mistake *noun* something that is wrong
mystery *noun* something strange and puzzling that you do not understand

Nn
nibble *verb* take tiny bites of something
noise *noun* a sound that you can hear

Oo
overjoyed *adjective* very happy or delighted

Pp
pant *verb* take short, quick breaths because you have been moving quickly

Word Cloud dictionary

peck *verb* the motion a bird makes with its beak to touch something or pick it up

pedestrian *noun* someone who is walking along the street

peer *verb* look at someone or something closely or with difficulty

pipe cleaner *noun* a piece of narrow wire covered in soft material, used to hold things together in craft

post office *noun* a place where you post letters and parcels and can buy stamps

publish *verb* print and sell a book or magazine

puff *verb* breathe in and out quickly because you have been running or exercising

Rr

ranch *noun* a large farm where a lot of sheep, cows or horses are kept

rattly *adjective* making a series of quick, short sounds like a rattle

remote *adjective* a place that is far away from towns and cities

reward *noun* something that is given to someone because they have done something good or helpful

rock *verb* move gently backwards and forwards or from side to side

rush *verb* run or do something quickly

Ss

safety *noun* keeping safe and away from danger

satchel *noun* a bag you wear over your shoulder or on your back, especially for carrying books to and from school

scent *noun* a nice smell or perfume

Word Cloud dictionary

scissors *noun* a tool that you use for cutting paper or cloth

scrape *verb* rub something against a rough, hard or sharp object

shear *verb* cut hair very short or cut the wool of a sheep

shiny *adjective* glossy or polished; bright

shrug *verb* lift your shoulders up and down, usually to show that you do not know something or do not care about it

slip *verb* slide or accidentally fall over

smirking *adjective* smiling in a silly or smug way

smug *adjective* very pleased with yourself

snare *noun* a trap for catching animals

snatch *verb* take hold of something quickly and unexpectedly

sniff *verb* breathe in air noisily through the nose, or to smell something by sniffing

spring *verb* move quickly or suddenly

squeal *verb* shout or cry out in a high voice

stable *noun* a building in which horses are kept

stamp album *noun* a book in which collectors of postage stamps can display and store their stamps

steal *verb* take something from someone without permission

struggle *verb* try to get free, or find something difficult

swishing *noun* the quick movement of something through the air, which makes a soft sound

Tt

thief *noun* someone who steals things

tights *noun* clothing which fits tightly over the legs and lower body

tradition *noun* something people have done in the same way for a very long time as part of their culture

trance *noun* a dreamy or unconscious state, as if you are sleeping

trickle *verb* flow slowly or thinly

truly *adverb* do something in a true or faithful way

two-way radio *noun* a radio through which you can communicate in both directions

Uu
underground *adjective* under the ground

Ww
warning *noun* something said or written to warn someone

weave *verb* make cloth from threads or a basket from reeds or cane

whistle *verb* make a high sound by blowing air through your lips

whopper *noun* anything unusually big of its kind

windmill *noun* a building with large sails that move in the wind and use the power of the wind to make energy

withdraw *verb* take something away; take it back

wobbly *adjective* unsteady

100 High frequency words

A
a
about
all
an
and
are
as
asked
at

B
back
be
big
but
by

C
called
came
can

children
come
could

D
dad
day
do
don't
down

F
for
from

G
get
go
got

H
had
have
he

help
her
here
him
his
house

I
I
I'm
if
in
into
is
it
it's

J
just

L
like
little

look
looked

M
made
make
me
Mr
Mrs
mum
my

N
no
not
now

O
of
off
oh
old
on

100 High frequency words

one	so	this	we
out	some	time	went
P	**T**	to	were
people	that	too	what
put	the	**U**	when
S	their	up	will
said	them	**V**	with
saw	then	very	**Y**
see	there	**W**	you
she	they	was	your

100 High frequency words

A Find the nouns, verbs, adjectives and adverbs in the list of high frequency words and complete the chart below (some words might go into more than one group).

noun	verb	adjective	adverb

100 High frequency words

B Use a dictionary to help you find three words from the list of high frequency words that can be used in more than one word category. Then make sentences to show the different meanings. *Example*: saw

saw/*noun* I used the saw to cut off the branch from the tree.

saw/*verb* I saw a really interesting programme about dolphins last night.

1 _____

2 _____

3 _____

100 High frequency words

C Complete this table using the nouns from the list of high frequency words.

singular	plural
dad	dads

100 High frequency words

A Look at the verbs in the list of high frequency words. Divide them into the following two groups.

present	past
come	asked

B Choose five of the present tense verbs above and change them into the past tense. Then use the verbs in a sentence.

Example: come

My friend **came** to my house to ask if I wanted to go to the park with him.

1 _____

2 _____

3 _____

4 _____

5 _____

C Find the two question words in the list of high frequency words and use each of them to write a question about your favourite animal.

1 _____

2 _____

New Word List

English word	Home language word or English definition

New Word List

English word	Home language word or English definition